SCHOLASTIC

News

Nonfiction Readers

A Komodo Dragon Hatchling Grows Up

by Katie Marsico

Children's Press®
A Division of Scholastic Inc.
New York Toronto London Auckland Sydney
Mexico City New Delhi Hong Kong
Danbury, Connecticut

These content vocabulary word builders are for grades 1–2.

Subject Consultant: Susan H. Gray, MS, Zoology

Reading Consultant: Cecilia Minden-Cupp, PhD, Former Director of the Language and Literacy Program, Harvard Graduate School of Education, Cambridge, Massachusetts

Photographs © 2007: AP/Wide World Photos/Paul B. Southerland: 23 bottom right; Bruce Coleman Inc./Hans Reinhard: 23 top left; Corbis Images/Wolfgang Kaehler: back cover, 19; Getty Images/Photolibrary.com/ Photonica: 5 bottom right, 8 right; iStockphoto/Stephen Bonk: 23 bottom left; Minden Pictures: 5 bottom left, 9, 11, 20 top left (Tui De Roy), cover right inset, 2, 4 bottom right, 7, 20 top right, 21 top left (Cyril Ruoso/JH Editorial); Nature Picture Library Ltd./Michael Pitts: cover background, cover center inset, cover left inset, 1, top, 6, 13, 15, 20 bottom, 21 bottom; Peter Arnold Inc./Fred Bruemmer: 4 bottom left, 17, 21 top right; Photo Researchers, NY/E. R. Degginger: 8 left, 23 top right; Toronto Zoo: 4 top, 10, 20 center left.

Book Design: Simonsays Design!
Book Production: The Design Lab

Library of Congress Cataloging-in-Publication Data
Marsico, Katie, 1980–
    A komodo dragon hatchling grows up / by Katie Marsico.
       p. cm. — (Scholastic news nonfiction readers)
    Includes bibliographical references.
    ISBN-13: 978-0-531-17477-7
    ISBN-10: 0-531-17477-8
    1. Komodo dragon—Growth—Juvenile literature. 2. Komodo dragon—Development—Juvenile literature. I. Title. II. Series.
    QL666.L29M345 2007
    597.95'968—dc22   2006023797

1 2 3 4 5 6 7 8 9 10 R 16 15 14 13 12 11 10 09 08 07

CONTENTS

WORD HUNT

Look for these words as you read. They will be in **bold**.

embryos
(**em**-bree-ohz)

juvenile
(**joo**-vuh-nile)

Komodo dragon
(kuh-**mo**-do
drag-uhn)

hatch
(hach)

hatchlings
(**hach**-lings)

lizards
(**li**-zurdz)

reptiles
(**rep**-tylz)

5

Dragons!

Komodo dragons are the largest **lizards** in the world. Adults can grow to be 10 feet (3 meters) long. That is probably longer than your couch!

Did you know that these giant lizards **hatch** from eggs?

hatch

Komodo dragons live on just a few islands in Indonesia.

Komodo dragons, like all lizards, are **reptiles**. Reptiles are cold-blooded and lay eggs.

Cold-blooded animals have the same body temperature as their surroundings.

reptiles

Komodo dragons sit in the sun to keep warm.

Female Komodo dragons dig nests in the ground.

They usually lay between fifteen and thirty eggs.

The eggs contain **embryos**.

It takes eight to nine months for a Komodo dragon embryo to mature.

embryo

A female Komodo dragon sits outside her nest.

It is time for the eggs to hatch! The babies break out of their shells.

Komodo dragon **hatchlings** are between 12 and 18 inches (30 and 46 centimeters) long.

What do the babies do first? They scramble for the trees!

Why do you think Komodo dragon hatchlings head for the trees?

The trees help protect hatchlings from enemies, such as birds, snakes, and older, larger Komodo dragons.

A hatchling also learns to find food in the trees. It hunts and eats insects and smaller lizards.

Living in trees helps keep Komodo
dragon hatchlings safe.

A one-year-old Komodo dragon is called a **juvenile**.

Juvenile Komodo dragons spend time on the ground. They are now too large to climb many trees.

On the ground, Komodo dragons eat larger animals such as monkeys and deer.

A juvenile Komodo dragon eats a deer.

Life on the ground can be dangerous for the juveniles. Sometimes they are eaten by hungry adult Komodo dragons.

Juveniles that survive become adults between five and seven years old. Then they are ready for new Komodo dragon hatchlings of their own.

Komodo dragons can live to be more than fifty years old.

A KOMODO DRAGON HATCHLING GROWS UP!

1. A mother Komodo dragon lays her eggs in a nest in the ground.

2. A Komodo dragon embryo takes eight to nine months to mature.

3. Finally, the baby Komodo dragon hatches from its egg!

6 Juvenile Komodo dragons become adults between five and seven years old.

5

After about one year, the juveniles leave the trees and hunt on the ground.

4

The hatchlings head straight for the trees!

YOUR NEW WORDS

embryos (**em**-bree-ohz) babies that are
growing inside eggs

hatch (hach) to break out of an egg

hatchlings (**hach**-lings) baby animals,
such as Komodo dragons, that have just
hatched from their eggs

juvenile (**joo**-vuh-nile) a young person or
animal

Komodo dragon (kuh-**mo**-do **drag**-uhn)
the largest lizard in the world

lizards (**li**-zurdz) reptiles with long bodies,
four legs, and a tail

reptiles (**rep**-tylz) cold-blooded animals that
lay eggs

THESE ANIMALS ARE REPTILES, TOO!

alligator

crocodile

snake

turtle

INDEX

FIND OUT MORE

Book:
Eckart, Edana. *Komodo Dragon*. New York: Children's Press, 2003.

Website:
Woodland Park Zoo: The Dragons of Komodo
http://www.zoo.org/komodo/facts/facts.htm

MEET THE AUTHOR
Katie Marsico lives with her family outside of Chicago, Illinois. She has never seen a Komodo dragon up close and would much prefer reading about them in books.